ISBN 978-0-331-38610-3
PIBN 11116107

VOL. 8 No. 16

APRIL 18, 1958

Cooperative
ECONOMIC INSECT
REPORT

Issued by

PLANT PEST CONTROL DIVISION

AGRICULTURAL RESEARCH SERVICE

UNITED STATES DEPARTMENT OF AGRICULTURE

AGRICULTURAL RESEARCH SERVICE

PLANT PEST CONTROL DIVISION

PLANT PEST SURVEY SECTION

The Cooperative Economic Insect Report is issued weekly as a service to American Agriculture. Its contents are compiled from information supplied by cooperating State, Federal, and industrial entomologists and other agricultural workers. In releasing this material the Division serves as a clearing house and does not assume responsibility for accuracy of the material.

Reports and inquiries pertaining to this release should be mailed to:

Plant Pest Survey Section
Plant Pest Control Division
Agricultural Research Service
United States Department of Agriculture
Washington 25, D. C.

Volume 8   April 18, 1958   Number 16

COOPERATIVE ECONOMIC INSECT REPORT

Highlights of Insect Conditions

SPOTTED ALFALFA APHID increasing rapidly in areas of New Mexico. (p. 294).

Some heavy infestations of ARMY CUTWORM in western Nebraska. (p. 295).

APHID buildup continues in California citrus, new growth damaged. APPLE
APHID active in Knox County, Indiana. GREEN PEACH APHID hatching at
Wenatchee, Washington. (p. 296).

TOMATO PSYLLID and TOMATO FRUITWORM damaging tomatoes in lower Rio Grande
Valley, Texas. (p. 297).

Indications heaviest PEA APHID populations in several years at Walla Walla,
Washington. (p. 294).

GYPSY MOTH program for 1958. (p. 298).

JAPANESE BEETLE treatment at Fort Madison, Iowa and East St. Louis and
Sheldon, Illinois. (p. 299).

New record of HACKBERRY LACE BUG in Florida. (p. 299).

Some First Reported Records of Season: SWEETCLOVER WEEVIL active in South
Dakota. LYGUS BUG adults active in Delaware, Nebraska and Idaho. THREE-
CORNERED ALFALFA HOPPER appearing in Oklahoma. APPLE GRAIN APHID hatching
as far north as Massachusetts. PEAR PSYLLA laying eggs in New York.
MEXICAN BEAN BEETLE and BEAN LEAF BEETLE active in Georgia. CABBAGE MAGGOT
adults at Walla Walla, Washington. TENT CATERPILLARS appearing in Delaware
and Washington. PLUM CURCULIO on peach trees at Fort Valley, Georgia.

SUMMARY OF INSECT CONDITIONS - 1957 - California. (p. 303).

INSECTS not known to occur in United States. (p. 313).

****

Reports in this issue are for the week ending April 11, unless otherwise
designated.

WEATHER OF THE WEEK ENDING APRIL 14

Spring continued to lag in the southern two-thirds of the country with the
return of the cold, wet weather pattern of March. The week brought more than
an inch of moisture to much of the lower Great Plains and East, and temperatures
for the week averaged 6° to 9° below normal in the Appalachian region and south
central portion of the country, with extreme departures of 12° below normal at
Oklahoma City, Oklahoma, and 14° at Amarillo, Texas. Farmwork, generally
ranged from 1 to 3 weeks later than normal. In contrast, the season is 2 to
3 weeks early in many sections from the Great Lakes to the Pacific Coast where
the week was abnormally warm and dry. A high pressure ridge of cold air,
which extended down through the midcontinent area at the beginning of the period
and drifted slowly eastward during the remainder of the week, was responsible
for frost and freezing as far south as central Mississippi and the Carolinas.
On the 8th, a low of 28° was recorded at Corinth, Mississippi, where the
probability of this low temperature on this late date is once in 25 years.
Temperatures moderated during the latter part of the period and daily maxima
over the weekend rose into the 70's in the South and in the 60's as far
North as the Great Lakes and southern New England.

A dying storm over the Northeast brought mostly light amounts of rain and
snow to the Ohio Valley and Northeast on the 7th. But most of the heavy
precipitation in the South and East occurred from the 9th through the 12th
during the passage of a storm from the northern Gulf up the Atlantic Coast.
Some unusually heavy rains were recorded in the Southeast during this storm.
Apalachicola, Florida, recorded 7.60 inches on the morning of the 10th, the
heaviest April 24-hour total there in the past 35 years. One to 9 inches of
snow fell in parts of the Northeast. New record amounts for so late in the
season included 5 and 7 inches at Hartford and Storrs, Connecticut,
respectively, and 4 inches at Providence, Rhode Island. Although this new
snow soon melted, the cover remained heavy in parts of northern New England
where Greenville, Maine, measured 31 inches on the 14th. A low pressure
area in the far Southwest was responsible for light to moderate showers
there on the 7th and throughout most of the Rocky Mountain region and lower
and western Great Plains on the 8th, with daily precipitation continuing
in the western portions of the central and northern Great Plains until the
weekend. Rains at San Francisco, California, on the 7th ended a period of
daily rains there which began on March 27, the longest such period on record
there for so late in the season in 109 years. Also, San Francisco has
recorded 5.44 inches of rain since April 1, already the wettest April since
1884. Snowfall in the western Great Plains ranged up to 6 inches in eastern
Colorado and western Kansas, and up to 2 feet on the eastern slopes of the
mountains of northeastern New Mexico. Light to heavy rains were falling in
the lower Great Plains again at the end of the period. (Summary supplied
by U. S. Weather Bureau).

WEATHER BUREAU 30-DAY OUTLOOK

MID-APRIL TO MID-MAY 1958

The Weather Bureau's 30-day outlook for the period mid-April to mid-May calls
for temperatures to average above seasonal normals over the northern half of
the nation with greatest unseasonal warmth over the Great Lakes Region and
Upper Mississippi Valley. Slightly below normal temperatures are expected to
prevail over the southern third of the country except above normal in California.
In the remaining area about normal averages are in prospect. Precipitation
is expected to exceed normal over the southern half of the nation from the
Southern Rocky Mountain States eastward to the Atlantic Seaboard, and also in
the Pacific Northwest. Subnormal rainfall with considerable sunshine is
indicated over the northern half of the nation and also in the far Southwest.
(Namias)

CEREAL AND FORAGE INSECTS

GRASSHOPPERS - OKLAHOMA - First-instar nymphs at Stillwater, March 31.
(Bieberdorf). NEBRASKA - Some eggs of Melanoplus bilituratus and M. differen-
tialis in southeastern areas are in segmentation stage. (Andersen). NEW
MEXICO - Overwintering adults and nymphs becoming active in Quay and Curry
Counties. (N. Mex. Coop. Rept.).

EUROPEAN CORN BORER (Pyrausta nubilalis) - SOUTH DAKOTA - Field survival in
17 eastern counties averaged 84 percent. (Hantsbarger). NORTH DAKOTA -
Winter survival averages 78 percent in southeastern corn-growing counties.
(N. D. Ins. Rept.).

GREENBUG (Toxoptera graminum) - ALABAMA - Damage to wheat in Autauga County.
Infestations spotted, counts ranging from 4 to 15-25 per 10 sweeps in same
field. (Grimes). OKLAHOMA - Very light numbers in small grains in east and east-
central counties. (Coppock). Found in only 1 field in Caddo County, 0-10
per linear foot. (Henderson). NEW MEXICO - Light on barley in Chaves County.
(N. Mex. Coop. Rept.). TEXAS - No apparent spread from spot infestations in
numberous volunteer small grain fields in north central areas. (Chada).
Medium to heavy on oats in Delta County.(Hawkins). KANSAS - None found in
small grains examined in 12 southeastern counties. (Matthew).

SOUTHWESTERN CORN BORER (Zeadiatraea grandiosella) - OKLAHOMA - Mortality
of overwintered larvae in a Payne County field was 22 percent. Four living
larvae were summer form (spotted). (Arbuthnot).

WINTER GRAIN MITE (Penthaleus major) - OKLAHOMA - Up to 50 per linear foot
in small grains in Creek County. (Coppock). Heavy population (hundreds per
foot) in a field of volunteer wheat near Hydro, Caddo County. (Henderson).
KANSAS - Very light, 3-24 per linear foot, in a few wheat and barley fields
in 5 southeastern counties. (Matthew).

ENGLISH GRAIN APHID (Macrosiphum granarium) - OKLAHOMA - Very light in east
central and eastern counties. (Coppock). Populations in Caddo County low
(0-125 per linear foot) but generally distributed. Most fields averaged
0-10 per foot. (Henderson). DELAWARE - Common on ryegrass in central Sussex
County, small numbers elsewhere. (MacCreary, Conrad). TEXAS - Present in
small grain fields in north central area, confined mostly to lower leaves
and damage slight. (Chada). KANSAS - Non-economic infestations in nearly
all wheat and barley fields examined in 11 southeastern counties. (Matthew).

CORN LEAF APHID (Rhopalosiphum maidis) - TEXAS - Infesting wheat and barley
in Kaufman County. (Hawkins).

A CHRYSOMELID (Myochrous sp.) TEXAS - Feeding on corn in Brazoria County.
(Turney).

A FLEA BEETLE - TEXAS - Damaging seedling corn in Navarro County. (Burleson).

MITES and APHIDS - UTAH - Mites numerous on pasture lands at La Verkin,
Washington County, and aphids causing some damage to small grains in the county.
(Knowlton).

LEAFHOPPERS - FLORIDA - Graminella nigrifrons averaged 9 per 75 sweeps on
rice at Belle Glade. (Fla. Coop. Surv.). UTAH - Numerous in alfalfa fields
and roadside grass in Cache County. (Knowlton).

PALE WESTERN CUTWORM (Agrotis orthogonia) - NEBRASKA - Averaged 1 per linear
foot in 1 field in western Keith County. None found in Deuel, Perkins or
Garden Counties. (Pruess).

PEA APHID (Macrosiphum pisi) - MARYLAND - Averaged 3 per 10 sweeps in Talbot County alfalfa. (U. Md., Ent. Dept.). OKLAHOMA - Increasing rapidly in eastern alfalfa fields, with counts up to 350 per 10 sweeps. (Coppock). DELAWARE - Common on alfalfa. (MacCreary, Conrad). NEBRASKA - Extremely light population appearing in southern Nemaha and Richardson Counties.(McKnight, Andersen). NEW MEXICO - Light infestations on alfalfa throughout southern area. (N. Mex. Coop. Rept.). IDAHO - Active on alfalfa in Canyon County, March 28. (Waters). Few observed in many sampled alfalfa fields. (Gittins). TEXAS - Two per 10 sweeps on alfalfa in Delta County. (Hawkins). KANSAS - Present in nearly all older established alfalfa stands in 11 southeast counties. Counts non-economic, ranging 2-200 per 25 sweeps. Few adults in 1 seedling alfalfa field in Cowley County. (Simpson). WASHINGTON - Averaging 125 per 100 tips in alfalfa indicating heaviest population in the Walla Walla area in several years. (Cook).

SPOTTED ALFALFA APHID (Therioaphis maculata) - OKLAHOMA - None found in several east central and eastern counties. (Coppock). No increase in Payne County. (Bieberdorf). NEW MEXICO - Increasing rapidly in Lea, Chaves, Eddy, Otero and Dona Ana Counties. (N. Mex. Coop. Rept.). KANSAS - None found in alfalfa in 12 southeastern and 3 north central counties. (Simpson).

CLOVER LEAF WEEVIL (Hypera punctata) - MARYLAND - Moderate larval damage to red clover at Easton, Talbot County. (U. Md.,Ent. Dept.). IDAHO - Readily found in alfalfa and red clover fields in southwest on April 1. Many larvae over half-grown, averaging 2-15 per crown. (Waters). In Boise Valley populations occasionally reach 10 larvae per plant in some fields. Larvae found in all fields examined from Grand View to Jerome but in very low numbers. (Gittins). KANSAS - Found in nearly all old established alfalfa stands in 12 southeastern counties. Larvae averaged 1-9 per crown with 40 percent showing apparent fungus disease. (Matthew).

ALFALFA WEEVIL (Hypera postica) - MARYLAND - Few larvae and 1 adult taken from alfalfa in Talbot County. Activity low due to wet cool weather. (U. Md., Ent. Dept.). DELAWARE - Very little change, first and second-instar larvae feeding lightly on alfalfa throughout State. (MacCreary, Conrad). IDAHO - Light injury in most fields in Payette, Homedale, Grand View and Jerome areas apparently due to adult feeding. Adults active in Rupert area on April 9 and first eggs found. (Gittins). NORTH CAROLINA - Small to medium-sized larvae in alfalfa throughout the Piedmont area. (Farrier).

SWEETCLOVER WEEVIL (Sitona cylindricollis) - SOUTH DAKOTA - Adults active in sweetclover fields in east central and southeastern regions. Some areas show heavy feeding damage on young emerging plants. (Hantsbarger).

TARNISHED PLANT BUG (Lygus lineolaris) - OKLAHOMA - Overwintering adults averaged 5-35 per 10 sweeps in alfalfa in Creek and Tulsa Counties but lighter in other eastern counties. (Coppock). DELAWARE - Few adults on alfalfa in eastern Sussex County. (MacCreary, Conrad). NEBRASKA - Light in southeastern counties, 5-7 per 100 sweeps. (Andersen).

LYGUS BUGS (Lygus spp.) - NEW MEXICO - Very numerous in alfalfa and grain fields near Tucumcari, Quay County. (N. Mex. Coop. Rept.). IDAHO - L. hesperus and L. elisus adults active in most alfalfa fields sampled but overwintering populations very low. (Gittins).

GREEN CLOVERWORM (Plathypena scabra) - ALABAMA - Light in crimson clover in Autauga County. No activity in Chambers, Randolph and Tallapoosa Counties. (Grimes).

CUTWORMS - IDAHO - Occasional specimens in legumes sampled from Weiser to Jerome. (Gittins). UTAH - Damaging pastures at Hurricane, Washington County. (Hughes, Knowlton).

CUCUMBER BEETLES (Diabrotica spp.) - KANSAS - Single specimen taken in alfalfa fields in each of Cowley, Montgomery and Labette Counties. (Matthew).

CLOVER ROOT CURCULIO (Sitona hispidula) - IDAHO - Adults in very low numbers in most alfalfa fields sampled from Weiser to Jerome. (Gittins).

ARMY CUTWORM (Chorizagrotis auxiliaris) - NEBRASKA - Populations heavy in western Keith and eastern Deuel Counties. Few fields average 5 per linear foot in winter wheat and barley, most averaged 0.2-3.0. (Pruess). KANSAS - None found in small grains and alfalfa in 12 southeastern counties. (Matthew).

APPLE GRAIN APHID (Rhopalosiphum fitchii) - OKLAHOMA - Light to medium (20-150 per linear foot) in widely scattered fields of wheat in eastern counties. (Coppock). Populations high (up to 1500 per linear foot) in occasional fields in Caddo County, but numbers small in most fields. (Henderson). TEXAS - Confined to lower leaves in north central small grain fields. Damage light. (Chada).

THREE-CORNERED ALFALFA HOPPER (Spissistilus festinus) - OKLAHOMA - First appearing this year in Tulsa, Muskogee and Sequoyah Counties, 0-3 per 10 sweeps. (Coppock). NEW MEXICO - Averaged 15-20 per 100 sweeps in alfalfa near Tularosa, Otero County. (N. Mex. Coop. Rept.).

VEGETABLE WEEVIL (Listroderes costirostris obliquus) - CALIFORNIA - Heavy infestation damaging alfalfa plantings in Oso Valley, Santa Barbara County. (Cal. Coop. Rept.).

THRIPS - NEW MEXICO - Very abundant in alfalfa fields in Lea, Eddy and Chaves Counties. (N. Mex. Coop. Rept.).

ALFALFA CATERPILLAR (Colias philodice eurytheme) - OKLAHOMA - From 0-2 larvae per alfalfa crown in east central counties. (Coppock). IDAHO - Few half-grown larvae observed in alfalfa in Owyhee County. (Gittins).

SOYBEAN CYST NEMATODE (Heterodera glycines) - Sampling in KENTUCKY was negative. One new field found in Pemiscot County, Missouri. (PPC, Cent. Reg., Mar. Rept.).

FRUIT INSECTS

EUROPEAN RED MITE (Panonychus ulmi) - ILLINOIS - None hatching at Carbondale. (Meyer, Apr. 9). INDIANA - Eggs not hatching at Vincennes. (Hamilton, Apr. 8). NEW YORK - Eggs plentiful in orchards in Orleans County. (N. Y. Wkly. Rept.).

TWO-SPOTTED SPIDER MITE (Tetranychus telarius) - WASHINGTON - Heavy concentration of overwintered females on apple buds in orchards at Monitor, Chelan County. (Hoyt).

CLOVER MITE (Bryobia praetiosa complex) - NEW MEXICO - Larvae and nymphs abundant on unsprayed trees in fruit-growing areas of Otero, Lincoln and De Baca Counties. (N. Mex. Coop. Rept.). IDAHO - Becoming active and migrating from winter hibernating quarters to host plants. (Gibson, Manis). UTAH - Not too numerous on apple trees at Kanosh and Fillmore. (Knowlton, Richenbach).

EYE-SPOTTED BUD MOTH (Spilonota ocellana) - WASHINGTON - Larvae tying foliage and causing considerable feeding injury on apple at Wawawai on April 2. (Johansen).

PLUM CURCULIO (Conotrachelus nenuphar) - GEORGIA - First adults, 1 male and 1 female, taken on peach trees April 2. No egg development in female, therefore no egg deposition expected for several weeks. (Snapp). LOUISIANA - Extremely scarce on wild plum in northern area. (Newsom, Spink).

LEAF CRUMPLER (Acrobasis indigenella) - CALIFORNIA - Medium infestation on
apricot and plum trees at Chula Vista, San Diego County. (Cal. Coop. Rept.).

CATFACING INSECTS - ILLINOIS - Lygus lineolaris active on peaches; 25 jarred
from 10 trees at Carbondale. One stink bug jarred. (Meyer).

APHIDS - ILLINOIS - Beginning first molt on apples at Carbondale. (Meyer).
INDIANA - Aphis pomi hatching in Knox County, April 1; readily found on buds.
(Hamilton). Heavy on apples at Orleans. (Marshall). DELAWARE -Newly hatched
Rhopalosiphum fitchii on apple buds in Kent and Sussex Counties. (MacCreary,
Conrad, Apr. 8). NEW MEXICO - Eriosoma lanigerum caused considerable damage to
roots of apple trees at Hondo, Lincoln County. Myzus persicae appearing on
peach trees at Roswell, Chaves County. (N. Mex. Coop. Rept.). WASHINGTON -
Myzus persicae eggs hatching on peach trees in Wenatchee area. (Anthon,
Feb. 25). NEW JERSEY - R. fitchii eggs hatching on apple. (Ins.-Dis. News).
CALIFORNIA - New growth of citrus damaged in several counties. Potentially
serious buildup, due to early appearance and high populations. Biological
control achieved in Los Angeles and Riverside Counties. Chemical control
applied in addition to biological control in Highgrove area of San Bernardino
County. (Cal. Coop. Rept.). MASSACHUSETTS - R. fitchii hatching in earliest
areas. (Crop Pest Control Mess.). NEW YORK - First R. fitchii noted April 8
in Ulster County, and on April 10 in Orange County. Myzus cerasi hatched in
numbers on April 10 in Orange County. (N.Y. Wkly. Rept.).

PEACH TREE BORER (Sanninoidea exitiosa) - ALABAMA - Heavy infestations in
Chambers and Randolph Counties with some trees seriously injured. (Grimes).

PEACH TREE BORERS - UTAH - Numerous in stone fruits in Washington County.
(Knowlton, Hughes, Apr. 5).

PEACH TWIG BORER (Anarsia lineatella) - WASHINGTON - Larvae burrowing tips of
twigs and buds of peach at Wawawai. (Johansen, Apr. 2).

PEAR PSYLLA (Psylla pyricola) - NEW YORK - Adults laying eggs on April 10 in
Orleans County, and eggs found on April 13 in Wayne County. (N.Y. Wkly. Rept.).

ROUNDHEADED APPLE TREE BORER (Saperda candida) - ALABAMA - Light numbers in
large and weakened apple trees in Randolph County. (Grimes).

SAN JOSE SCALE (Aspidiotus perniciosus) - CALIFORNIA - Heavy populations on
prune trees in Hamilton City, Glenn County. (Cal. Coop. Rept.).

EASTERN SUBTERRANEAN TERMITE (Reticulitermes flavipes) - ALABAMA - Attacking
weak and dying peach and apple trees in Chambers and Randolph Counties.
(Grimes).

CUTWORMS - WASHINGTON- Active on peach trees during February in Wenatchee
area. (Anthon).

CALIFORNIA RED SCALE (Aonidiella aurantii) - CALIFORNIA - Medium to heavy
on lemon trees at Dinuba, Tulare County. (Cal. Coop. Rept.).

Citrus Insect Situation, First Week of April, Lake Alfred, Florida
Activity of PURPLE SCALE increased and will continue to increase for several
following weeks. Activity of FLORIDA RED SCALE unchanged but will increase
sharply next week, and continue to increase for several weeks. CITRUS RED
MITE activity increased with some further increase expected. CITRUS RUST
MITE activity declined and will continue to decline on old leaves through April.
SIX-SPOTTED MITE being found 'in increasing numbers on new foliage. APHIDS are
increasing and may be troublesome in some young groves and groves that

were severely frozen. (Pratt, Thompson, Johnson, April 8).

A MAY BEETLE (Phyllophaga praetermissa) - MISSISSIPPI - Destroying newly emerging pecan foliage in Pike County. (Hutchins).

TRUCK CROP INSECTS

BEET LEAFHOPPER (Circulifer tenellus) - CALIFORNIA - Winter host plants drying in Imperial Valley of Imperial County. Practically no leafhoppers found on west side of county were control applied. Slight increase in populations on east side of county. Average of one leafhopper per 100 sweeps in some fields; occasional leafhopper in flax. Leafhoppers collected from west side of county prior to control 20 percent viriliferous. Those from east side apparently not carriers. In San Joaquin Valley heavy rains stimulated growth of annuals causing an unfavorable breeding ground. (Cal. Coop. Rept.).

COLORADO POTATO BEETLE (Leptinotarsa decemlineata) - GEORGIA - Moderate infestations on tomatoes in Tattnall County (Johnson). FLORIDA - All stages infesting tomatoes and eggplants in Alachua County. (Fla. Coop. Surv.).

MEXICAN BEAN BEETLE (Epilachna varivestis) - GEORGIA - Light on snap and lima beans in Colquitt, Brooks, Lowndes and Tattnall Counties. (Johnson).

ONION MAGGOT (Hylemya antiqua) - WASHINGTON - Emergence of spring brood started during last of February and continued through March in Walla Walla area. Cool weather beginning mid-March resulted in delayed development and emergence of abnormally formed adults. (Woodworth).

SEED-CORN MAGGOT (Hylemya cilicrura) - WASHINGTON - Spring-brood emergence well along in Walla Walla area. Adults taken on sticky stakes were 8-9 times as numerous as same time in 1957. (Woodworth).

TOMATO FRUITWORM (Heliothis zea) - TEXAS - H. zea and Protoparce quinquemaculata infesting tomatoes in lower Rio Grande Valley. Large numbers of H. zea eggs being deposited. (Deer).

TOMATO PSYLLID (Paratrioza cockerelli) - TEXAS - Considerable damage to tomatoes in lower Rio Grande Valley in conjunction with a mite. (Deer).

APHIDS - FLORIDA - Major problem on truck crops in Manatee County area. (Fla. Coop. Surv.).

BEAN LEAF BEETLE (Cerotoma trifurcata) - GEORGIA - Light infestations on snap and lima beans in Colquitt, Brooks, Lowndes and Tattnall Counties. (Johnson).

LYGUS BUGS - WASHINGTON - Lygus hesperus and L. elisus attacking spinach in Walla Walla area. Some control applied. (Woodward).

GREEN PEACH APHID (Myzus persicae) - OKLAHOMA - Populations on spinach averaged 13.8 per leaf at Bixby, Tulsa County. (Walton). FLORIDA - Averaging 1-20 per potato plant at Hastings, St. Johns County, and La Crosse, Alachua County. (Fla. Coop. Surv.).

DIAMONDBACK MOTH (Plutella maculipennis) - GEORGIA - Infestations light to moderate on crucifers in Colquitt and Brooks Counties. (Johnson).

CABBAGE APHID (Brevicoryne brassicae) - GEORGIA - Light to heavy on cabbage and collards in Brooks County. (Johnson).

CABBAGE MAGGOT (Hylemya brassicae) - WASHINGTON - First adults in Walla Walla area taken on sticky boards during week ending April 1. (Woodward).

CYCLAMEN MITE (Stenotarsonemus pallidus) - WASHINGTON - Damaging strawberry plants some fields in Puyallup Valley which were heavily infested in 1957. (Breakey).

TOBACCO INSECTS

TOBACCO FLEA BEETLE (Epitrix hirtipennis) - GEORGIA - Light infestations on tobacco plant beds in Colquitt County. (Johnson).

CUTWORMS - GEORGIA - LIGHT infestations on tobacco in the field in Tattnall County. (Smith).

A GRASSHOPPER (Tettigidea prob. lateralis) - NORTH CAROLINA - Taken in tobacco plant bed in Pender County with evidence of damage. (Scott, Farrier).

GREEN PEACH APHID (Myzus persicae) - GEORGIA - Light to moderate infestations on tobacco plant beds in Tift, Colquitt, Brooks and Lowndes Counties. (Johnson).

COTTON INSECTS

Cotton Insects in Lower Rio Grande Valley, Texas: Cutworms are causing heavy damage in many fields. Darkling beetles causing some damage and spider mites are being found in more fields. A few aphids noted. (Deer).

FOREST, ORNAMENTAL AND SHADE TREE INSECTS

The 1958 Gypsy Moth Program

The 1958 gypsy moth (Porthetria dispar) program provides for: (a) spraying all known infestations outside the boundaries of the area of general infestation which involves eastern New York and New England; (b) spraying any "spot" infestations located within areas treated in 1956-57; (c) continued cooperation with the New England States in suppressing any infestations approaching outbreak proportions; (d) strict enforcement of quarantine regulations to prevent the spread of gypsy moths to other states and to protect from reinfestation areas treated in 1956 and 1957. The methods improvement program inaugurated in 1956 will be continued. Certain new chemicals show some promise of having a place in the gypsy moth program. These will be tested under field conditions in various formulations. Work aimed at the refinement of application equipment will be stressed. A comprehensive survey of all areas sprayed in 1956 and 1957 has proved the program successful beyond expectation. With limited "spotting-up" and adequate surveys with negative results it may be possible to relieve these areas of all quarantine regulations. Final plans for the current program in Pennsylvania have been worked out with our state cooperators. The eradication area in that State is in three parcels - a small area at Sterling; a small area in Promised Land east of Panther; and a larger area bounded by Wilkes-Barre, Stroudsburg, and Tamacqua. The area includes parts of Pike, Monroe, Carbon, Schuylkill, Wayne, Luzerne and Lackawanna Counties. Since programs in several of the other infested states may be carried out independently by the appropriate state agency or jointly with the Department, any inquiries should be referred to the proper officials of such states. (PPC, April 14)

BARK BEETLES (Dendroctonus spp.) - WEST VIRGINIA - Seriously injuring live red pine trees in Putnam County. (W. Va. Ins. Surv.).

A CYNIPID - TEXAS - Causing severe distortion to oak leaves in Brazos County, with 75 percent of leaves on some trees affected by galls. (Turney).

DEODAR WEEVIL (Pissodes nemorensis) - ALABAMA - Fairly common in Lee County pine trees. (Pearson).

EASTERN SPRUCE GALL APHID (Chermes abietis) - WISCONSIN - Galls numerous on Norway spruce in Two Rivers area of Manitowoc County. (Wis. Ins. Bul.).

EUROPEAN PINE SHOOT MOTH (Rhyaciona buoliana) - WISCONSIN - Larvae successfully overwintered but some mortality occurred. (Wis. Ins. Bul.).

IPS BEETLES (Ips spp.) - ALABAMA - Fairly large numbers of I. avulsus, I. grandicollis and I. calligraphus found in pine forests in Lee County. (Pearson). WEST VIRGINIA - Adults seriously injuring red pine in Jackson and Putnam Counties. (W. Va. Ins. Surv.).

Forest Insects, Arkansas: New IPS BEETLE activity reported from Stamps area of Lafayette County. BLACK TURPENTINE BEETLE infestations active on small scale in Calhoun County. Hatching of Neodiprion taedae linearis eggs has not been observed. PINE TIP MOTH adult emergence began in Hope area February 4 and has progressed steadily since, with heavy emergence in Union and Ashley Counties. No activity in northern areas. PINE WEBWORM infestations are present in Newton and Cleburne Counties. (Ark. For. Pest Rept., April)

LOCUST TWIG BORER (Ecdytolopha insiticiana) - ALABAMA - Heavy damage young locust in Lee County. (Pearson).

PINE MIDGES (Retinodiplosis spp.) - ALABAMA - R. resinicola rather common on both old and young pine trees (Guyton, April 4) and Retinodiplosis sp. attacking pine twigs in Lee County. As many as 35 specimens of the latter taken from functioning gall. (Pearson).

HACKBERRY LACE BUG (Corythucha celtidis) - FLORIDA - Collected on hackberry at Gainesville, Alachua County. Apparently a new record for the State. Det. R. F. Hussey. (Fla. Coop. Surv.).

SPRUCE APHID (Aphis abietina) - WASHINGTON - Abundant and damaging to spruce in southwestern area in March. (Cox).

TENT CATERPILLARS (Malacosoma spp.) - DELAWARE - First hatching of M. americanum eggs noted April 7 on wild cherry, Sussex County. (MacCreary, Conrad). TEXAS - M. americanum continues to cause defoliation in Houston County. (Turney). LOUISIANA - M. americanum abundant in Webster, Claiborne, Lincoln and Bienville Parishes. (Newson, Spink). WASHINGTON - First instar larvae of M. pluviale and M. disstria observed on alder and willow in isolated areas from Puyallup to Everett. M. pluviale began hatching about April 1 and M. disstria about April 7. (Dailey).

JAPANESE BEETLE (Popillia japonica) - The cooperative control program, involving 4,495 acres in the vicinity of East St. Louis, ILLINOIS, and 1,925 acres at Fort Madison, IOWA, was completed during March. The cooperative control program at Sheldon, ILLINOIS was completed on about April 10, and involved 8,195 acres. (PPC)

A SLUG (Arion ater) - OREGON - Causing serious damage to a nursery planting near Rockaway, Tillamook County. Normal baiting procedures have not proved effective. (Loring).

A HOLLY LEAF MINER (Phytomyza sp.) - MARYLAND - Moderate numbers on hollies at Easton, Talbot County. (U. Md., Ent. Dept.).

APHIDS and MITES - FLORIDA - High populations on plants this spring. (Fla. Coop. Surv.).

APHIDS - NEW MEXICO - Light to heavy infestations on tulips, iris and gladiolas. Macrosiphum rosae heavy in several counties. (N. Mex. Coop. Rept.). ALABAMA - Heavy infestation on pine twigs in Lee County. (Guyton, Pearson). IDAHO - M. rosae colonizing on roses in Twin Falls County, April 7. (Gibson).

INSECTS AFFECTING MAN AND ANIMALS

CATTLE GRUBS (Hypoderma spp.) - KANSAS - H. bovis collected from native cattle at Salina, Salina County, and Manhattan, Riley County. This confirms earlier reports of occurrence in northern area of the State. (Knapp). UTAH - Common in nearly all cattle herds in Millard County. (Knowlton). Averaged 8 per head in unsprayed cattle in Sanpete County. (Funk, Knowlton).

CATTLE LICE - TEXAS - Attacking livestock in Hall County. (Hooser). UTAH - Moderately numerous on beef cattle in Washington, Kane and Millard Counties. (Hughes, Knowlton).

SCREW-WORM (Callitroga hominivorax) - FLORIDA - Very few collected in the Manatee County area. (Fla. Coop. Surv.).

SHEEP KED (Melophagus ovinus) - UTAH - Numerous in herds in Millard and Sanpete Counties. (Knowlton, et al.).

STORED-PRODUCT INSECTS

BROAD-NOSED GRAIN WEEVIL (Caulophilus latenasus) - CALIFORNIA - Reported from El Centro, Imperial County, for the first time on cotton and barley. All previous records have been from avocado. (Cal. Coop. Rept.).

DERMESTIDS - NEW MEXICO - Heavy infestation in stored grass seed at Los Lunas, Valencia County. (N. Mex. Coop. Rept.). CALIFORNIA - Light infestation of Novelsis andersoni in oats at Needles, San Bernardino. First record for county. (Cal. Coop. Rept.).

KHAPRA BEETLE (Trogoderma granarium) - NEBRASKA - Initial inspections of 56 sites in Gage County were negative. WISCONSIN - One initial and one repeat inspection made; both were negative. SOUTH DAKOTA - Two feed mills and seed houses in Watertown and one in Sioux Falls were inspected. (PPC, Cent. Reg.; Mar. Rept.).

Stored-grain Pest Survey, Oklahoma: Inspection of 8 granaries of farm-stored grain in Sequoyah County showed 1 infestation of wheat to average more than 200 lesser grain borer, 75-100 saw-toothed grain beetles, above 100 red flour beetles and more than 200 flat grain beetles per quart of grain. Another infestation in wheat averaged 3-8 rice weevils, 20-40 lesser grain borers, an occasional saw-toothed grain beetle and 10-15 flat grain beetles per quart of grain. An infestation in oats showed 25-30 rice weevils, 25-30 lesser grain borers, 40-50 saw-toothed grain beetles, 12-15 flat grain beetles and 50 psocids per quart of grain. (Coppock).

BENEFICIAL INSECTS

Beneficial Insects in Alfalfa, New Mexico: Damsel bugs, lacewings, lady beetles and pirate bugs abundant in alfalfa fields in southern area. First record of Praon palitans overwintering in State. Parasitizing spotted alfalfa aphid near Las Cruces, Dona Ana County. (N. Mex. Coop. Rept.).

HONEY BEE (Apis mellifera) - NORTH CAROLINA - Reduction from 45 to 14 hives in an apiary in Caldwell County due to cold and consumption of a honey-dew which causes severe dysentery. (Stephen). CALIFORNIA - Flood waters have damaged 11 apiaries of 800 colonies in Ventura County. At least 1,500 queen-rearing nuclei were drowned in Colusa County. Many apiaries starving as bees have been prevented from gathering food by bad weather. Supplemental feeding impossible in many areas because of flood waters. (Cal. Coop. Rept.).

A KLAMATHWEED BEETLE (Chrysolina gemellata) - CALIFORNIA - Active on klamathweed in Tuolumne County. (Cal. Coop. Rept.).

LACEWINGS - OKLAHOMA - Adults appearing in Sequoyah County alfalfa, 0-3 per 10 sweeps. (Coppock).

MISCELLANEOUS INSECTS

Imported Fire Ant Eradication Program: Total acres treated in 9 states to April 4 - 167,768. In ALABAMA, block treatments have been completed in Wilcox and Perry Counties and in Aiken, Berkeley, Edgefield, Marion and Spartanburg Counties, SOUTH CAROLINA. Aerial applications under State contract at Monroe, LOUISIANA, were also completed. In NORTH CAROLINA, 700 acres were found infested at Tarawa Terrace, a Marine Corps housing project in Onslow County. (PPC, So. Reg.).

A MARCH FLY (Bibio sp., probably nervosus) - OREGON - Emerging and attracting attention in blossoming fruit orchards in Willamette Valley. (Capizzi, April 6).

TERMITES - GEORGIA - Many complaints of swarming in Peach County. (Snapp, April 2). OKLAHOMA - Beginning to swarm in Tulsa County. (Griffin). SOUTH DAKOTA - Infestation in a home in Davison County is first county record for termites. (Lofgren). NEW MEXICO - Extensive damage to a home in Harding County. (N. Mex. Coop. Rept.).

CORRECTIONS

CEIR 8(11):205 - Under peach for New Jersey, unit loss should read 100,000 bushels and market loss should read $250,000.

LIGHT TRAP COLLECTIONS

	Pseud. unip.	Agrot. yps.	Felt. subt.	Hel. zea	Perid. marg.	Prod. ornith.	Laph. frug.	Lox. simil.
ALABAMA(County)								
Lee 4/2-12	68	19						
FLORIDA(Counties)								
Alachua 4/4-11	1							
Gadsden 3/24-4/8	33	1						
LOUISIANA								
Baton Rouge 4/4-10	4	3	3	5	4			
Franklin 4/2-8	4	1	1		1			
MISSISSIPPI								
Meridian 4/4	1							
Senatobia 4/8-11	36	2						
State College 4/4	1							
*Stoneville	171	28	1	2	74	1		
SOUTH CAROLINA(County)								
Charleston 4/7-13	7				5	1		
Oconee 4/5-11	19	2			3	7		
TENNESSEE(Counties)								
Blount 4/1-7	11	4			2	5		
Cumberland					1			
Greene						˙		
Madison	4				8			
Robertson	1							
TEXAS								
Brownsville 3/29-4/4	17	24	516	67	71		24	156
Waco 4/5-11	172		37	1	120	5		

*Four traps at Stoneville

SUMMARY OF INSECT CONDITIONS - 1957

CALIFORNIA

Compiled by A. G. Forbes

Highlights: SPOTTED ALFALFA APHID continued to spread over the State being reported for the first time in 6 counties. A FROSTED SCALE (Lecanium pruinosum) was reported for the first time in Shasta County infesting walnuts. SPRUCE NEEDLE MINER, new to the State, was found in Modoc County. The range of WALNUT HUSK FLY was extended into Santa Clara County and was reported for the first time from Merced and Stanislaus Counties. First infestations of PEAR PSYLLA were reported from Alameda, Solano, Sacramento and Yolo Counties. A PLANT BUG (Neoborus illitus) was taken for the first time in San Luis Obispo County, as were 2 carnation pests in Alameda County. SWEETCLOVER WEEVIL was collected in Alpine, Mono and Modoc Counties for first State records; some local damage. Other new county records were LESSER CLOVER LEAF WEEVIL in Mendocino and Alpine Counties, FALSE CHINCH BUG on black walnuts in Merced County, SMALL EUROPEAN ELM BARK BEETLE in Sacramento County, DARK-BROWN SPRUCE APHID in El Dorado County and RHODES-GRASS SCALE in Imperial County. CABBAGE LOOPER became one of the most important insects attacking vegetable crops in Los Angeles County. CITRUS RED MITE was number one pest of citrus in Orange and San Bernardino Counties. CRICKETS and GRASSHOPPERS did over $4,000,000 damage to agricultural crops in Imperial County.(Loss figures listed at end of Summary.)

Cereal and Forage Insects: SPOTTED ALFALFA APHID (Therioaphis maculata) continued to spread over the State, being found for the first time during 1957 in Mendocino, Siskiyou, Lassen, Lake, Sonoma and El Dorado Counties. Infestations and damage ranged from very light in Lassen County to heavy in San Diego County. Reported by counties as one of the most important insect pests for 1957 with a state-wide loss value of $9,704,627. LESSER CLOVER LEAF WEEVIL (Hypera nigrirostris) (see highlights). ALFALFA WEEVIL (Hypera postica) was the most injurious insect in the northeast area costing an estimated $120,760 in damages and controls. Populations ranged from medium to heavy and were light to medium in Siskiyou and Shasta Counties. In Siskiyou County CLOVER LEAF WEEVIL (H. punctata) ranged to heavy on alfalfa. SWEETCLOVER WEEVIL (Sitona cylindricollis) (see highlights). CLOVER ROOT CURCULIO (S. hispidula) was light to medium on Siskiyou County alfalfa. ARMYWORMS caused some damage to alfalfa in San Benito County and to alfalfa and tomatoes in Contra Costa County. Populations were light generally in the Sacramento Valley but heavy locally in alfalfa.

WESTERN YELLOW-STRIPED ARMYWORM (Prodenia praefica) was of concern in 3 northern counties, lightly damaging native shrubs and grasses during May. Alfalfa was damaged in Merced County. VARIEGATED CUTWORM (Peridroma margaritosa) infestations on alfalfa were general, varying to medium, in the 3 north central counties. GRANULATE CUTWORM (Feltia subterranea) was locally heavy on alfalfa in San Joaquin County. BEET ARMYWORM (Laphygma exigua) became a problem in the western side of Stanislaus County on alfalfa and was light to heavy locally in southern areas.

GRASSHOPPERS varied in importance over the State in 1957 attacking a wide range of crops. Damage estimates varied from as little as $500 to pasture in Plumas County to more than $500,000 in 3 of the mid-coastal counties. BROWN WHITE MITE (Petrobia latens) was medium on range grasses in Siskiyou County and caused an estimated $10,000 loss to Modoc County barley. PEA APHID (Macrosiphum pisi) was of local concern on alfalfa in various areas of the Sacramento Valley and ranged to moderate generally in 4 southern counties. CLOVER APHID (Anuraphis bakeri) built up in western Stanislaus County red clover in midsummer. LEAF

MINER damage was locally heavy on alfalfa in September in the Modesto area.
APHID vectors of yellow dwarf virus of barley and oats cost an estimated
$100,000 in control and damage on 122,754 acres in San Luis Obispo County.
The disease was less prevalent in 1957 in spite of a 40 percent increase in
barley acreage. LYGUS BUGS (Lygus spp.) were of concern on alfalfa in several
counties. Some heavy damage was recorded in Siskiyou and Tulare Counties.
Alfalfa, clover and other crops were damaged in the Sacramento Valley. Infestations ranged medium to heavy in 4 southern counties. MIRIDS (Irbisia spp.)
were medium to heavy in Lassen and Modoc Counties with severe mottling on about
40 acres of intermediate wheatgrass. A RICE LEAF MINER (Hydrellia griseola)
infested rice in Yolo, Yuba and Glenn Counties, doing $15,000 damage in the
latter county.

Fruit Insects (General): PEAR PSYLLA (Psylla pyricola) eggs occurred in nearly
all pear orchards in southwestern Mendocino County and the insect was recorded
for the first time in Alameda County. Moderate damage occurred in 1 orchard in
Santa Clara County, with more serious damage in Napa County where a loss of
$12,000 was reported. Heavy infestations in Lake County prevented fruit
packing in 2 orchards. Yolo, Sacramento and Solano Counties were infested for
the first time in 1957, all infestations being light. Medium populations of
RED-HUMPED CATERPILLAR (Schizura concinna) caused some concern on walnuts in
southern Mendocino County. Populations on walnuts in the Sacramento Valley
were above normal in two counties and general in one. Populations of CODLING
MOTH (Carpocapsa pomonella) ranging to medium, attacked pear, apple and cherry
in the Shasta Valley of Siskiyou County. Infestations ranged from light to
heavy on the walnuts and deciduous fruits in the southern part of the State,
particularly in untreated plantings. Infestations became a problem on walnuts
in Stanislaus County. In approximately 50 percent of the central coastal areas
moderate to severe damage occurred on apple, pear and walnut crops. Control
costs and losses exceeded $600,000 in this area; the greatest loss, $300,000,
occurred in Contra Costa County. Deciduous fruits and nuts were damaged in the
Sacramento Valley.

LESSER APPLEWORM (Grapholitha prunivora) was light to medium on apple and cherry
in the north central area. ORIENTAL FRUIT MOTH (G. molesta) gave considerable
trouble in northwest Tulare County in peaches and was generally light over the
county. The pest was locally light on deciduous fruit in southern areas. PEAR-
SLUG (Caliroa cerasi) infestations were medium in north central areas. PEACH
TWIG BORER (Anarsia lineatella) was distributed state-wide in 1957. Almonds,
apricots and peaches suffered an estimated $90,000 in damage in Contra Costa
County. Deciduous fruits and nuts were damaged in the Sacramento Valley.
Infestations were generally heavy in peach orchards of Stanislaus and Merced
Counties as well as in almond nuts in the latter county. A FROSTED SCALE
(Lecanium pruinosum) was reported for the first time in Shasta County. Light
or local infestations were reported on walnuts and almonds in other areas.
EUROPEAN FRUIT LECANIUM (L. corni) was general on prune, apricots and pears
in Napa County. Damage was estimated at $75,000 in San Benito County. Infes-
tations were of concern in areas of San Joaquin, Los Angeles, and San
Bernardino Counties also. CALICO SCALE (L. cerasorum) was heavy in many
orchards in the Carneros area of Napa County. Infestations of WALNUT APHID
(Chromaphis juglandicola) were general and caused $162,000 in damage and loss
in most of the central coastal counties locally damaged walnut orchards in
Sutter, Yolo and Sacramento Counties and were general in walnut orchards of
Santa Barbara, Los Angeles and Ventura Counties, requiring extensive treatment
in the latter county to hold down damage. WALNUT HUSK FLY (Rhagoletis
completa) extended its range into Santa Clara County infesting black walnuts in
the vicinity of Campbell and was reported for the first time in adjoining Merced
and Stanislaus Counties on the same host. Infestations ranged from light to

heavy in southern areas, Los Angeles County reporting little treatment due to a light crop and Ventura County experiencing heavy populations because of omitted treatment. Trapping surveys indicated a gradual northern extension of range along the coast.

CYCLAMEN MITE (Steneotarsonemus pallidus) was of considerable economic importance in strawberry-producing counties. Severe and general populations occurred in Santa Cruz and Santa Clara Counties. Alameda, Monterey and San Luis Obispo submitted an aggregate total of $1,736,000 for control and losses. In east central counties PEAR LEAF BLISTER MITE (Eriophyes pyri) and PEAR RUST MITE (Epitrimerus pyri) did damage in excess of $152,000 and localized heavy populations caused considerable russeting in San Diego County. TWO-SPOTTED SPIDER MITE (Tetranychus telarius) caused damage, mostly local, to fruit in several areas. Light to heavy infestations damaged almonds and grapes in San Joaquin County. PACIFIC SPIDER MITE (T. pacificus) was also of concern in some areas. Tetranychus mcdanieli, new to San Bernardino County, heavily damaged apple foliage in that county. EUROPEAN RED MITE (Panonychus ulmi) was general on deciduous fruits and walnuts in the central coastal area, 6 counties reporting moderate to severe damage and Sonoma County $107,500 for damage and control on apples, pears and prunes. Some peach orchards were severely damaged in Stanislaus County. Walnuts required extensive treatment in Ventura County.

CLOVER MITE (Bryobia praetiosa) was locally significant in San Luis Obispo County and the east central border counties. Loss and control in San Joaquin County was estimated at $342,000. Infestations were light to locally severe in the Sacramento Valley and light to medium in San Bernardino County. GRAPE ERINEUM MITE (Eriophyes vitis) was general in Napa County causing an estimated $135,000 damage to grapes. PEACH SILVER MITE (Vasates cornutus) was light to medium in San Joaquin County and Eotetranychus willamettei was of some significance on grapes in the Lodi area of this county. An AVOCADO MITE (Oligonychus punicae) was light to medium in 3 southern avocado-growing counties, with slight damage in San Diego County.

PEAR THRIPS (Taeniothrips inconsequens) was medium to heavy on prunes in the Gilroy area of Santa Clara County, with damage to prunes and pears in Napa County estimated at $20,000. APHIDS were reported throughout Tulare County on walnuts and citrus in light to severe infestations. ROSY APPLE APHID (Anuraphis roseus) caused $150,000 loss in Sonoma County. MEALY PLUM APHID (Hyalopterus arundinis) infestations were general in Sutter and Yolo Counties on prune. GREEN PEACH APHID (Myzus persicae) caused an estimated $55,000 loss to the Merced County peach crop. The latter two aphids did considerable damage to Napa County deciduous fruits. WOOLLY APPLE APHID (Eriosoma lanigerum) did considerable damage in Napa and Sonoma Counties and attacked apple and pear trees in the Placer County area. HOP APHID (Phorodon humuli) was general on prune in Sonoma County with losses estimated at $25,000. Medium populations of MELON APHID (Aphis gossypii) attacked melons around Victorville in San Bernardino County. Some other aphids of local or area importance in 1957 were APPLE APHID (Aphis pomi) generally distributed in Napa and Sonoma Counties with an estimated $100,000 in damage in the latter; BLACK PEACH APHID (Anuraphis persicae-niger) light generally; and a PEAR ROOT APHID (Eriosoma languinosum) damaging pear and apple nursery stock in Sacramento County.

SAN JOSE SCALE (Aspidiotus perniciosus) was general and severe in Lake and Santa Clara Counties attacking pears, peaches and cherries and important on deciduous fruits in Sutter and Tehama Counties. San Joaquin Valley losses were estimated at $639,264. Heavy infestations were reported in Stanislaus and Merced County peaches and light to heavy damage occurred on fruits and almonds in other areas. GRAPE MEALYBUG (Pseudococcus maritimus) damage to grapes varied from light to severe in Tulare, Kern, San Joaquin and Fresno Counties. Olives were lightly damaged by OLEANDER SCALE (Aspidiotus hederae) and lightly infested generally by BLACK SCALE (Saissetia oleae) in Tulare County.

The latter scale was considered very important on this host in Tehama County.
SOFT SCALE (Coccus hesperidum) was locally heavy in Napa County and light to
moderate on almonds in the Linden area of San Joaquin County. OLIVE SCALE
(Parlatoria oleae) infested olives and deciduous fruits in several counties.
Locally heavy infestations of WALNUT SCALE (Aspidiotus juglans-regiae) were
noted on walnut and peach in 2 southern counties. LONG-TAILED MEALYBUG
(Pseudococcus adonidum) was prevalent in San Diego County avocado groves, but
was not a problem.

GRASSHOPPERS required treatment or caused loss in Fresno County on citrus and
deciduous fruits. Moderate populations developed in eastern Stanislaus
County grape vineyards in June and Madera County experienced damage to all
crops. JUNE BEETLE (Cotinis texana) caused light damage on deciduous fruit in
Riverside and San Diego Counties. TENT CATERPILLARS (Malacosoma spp.) did an
estimated $10,000 damage to Napa County prunes and $40,000 damage to the prune
and apple crops in Sonoma County. WESTERN PEACH TREE BORER (Sanninoidea
exitiosa graefi) was of considerable significance attacking prune, peach,
apricot and almond, with San Benito and Contra Costa Counties giving a total of
$55,000 in losses. YELLOW-NECKED CATERPILLAR (Datana ministra) was general and
severe on apricots in Santa Clara County. SHOT-HOLE BORER (Scolytus rugulosus)
caused local heavy damage to drought-stricken deciduous fruit trees in San Diego
County. NAVEL ORANGEWORM (Paramyelois transitella) infestation in almond nuts
was generally moderate over Merced County. GRAPE LEAF FOLDER (Desmia funeralis)
ranged light to severe in Madera, Stanislaus, San Joaquin and Merced Counties.
AMERICAN PLUM BORER (Euzophera semifuneralis) moderately damaged almond,
nectarine and apricot trees in Madera County and required treatment. A GRAPE
LEAFHOPPER (Erythroneura elegantula) was troublesome in Tulare, Madera and San
Joaquin Counties. FALSE CHINCH BUG (Nysius ericae) caused considerable damage
to non-bearing walnuts in Merced County. A BUPRESTID (Chrysobothris mali) was
general in Placer County doing some $1,200 damage to apple, peach and other
young fruit trees. A SAWFLY (Hartigia cressonii) attacked and damaged an estimated
50 percent of raspberry canes in a single area of Calaveras County.

Citrus Insects: SOFT SCALE (Coccus hesperidum) attacked citrus along coastal
Santa Barbara County and was general in Tulare and Los Angeles Counties.
COTTONY-CUSHION SCALE (Icerya purchasi) infestations were generally light to
medium over Tulare County, with serious populations developing in the Coachella
Valley of Riverside County. Damage by CITRUS RED MITE (Panonychus citri) was
light to severe generally in Tulare County. Citrus red mite damage was light
to heavy and extensive in southern counties where treatment was lacking or late.
Early populations were low in some areas but built up markedly in the fall.
Nearly $3,000,000 in losses are attributed to this mite through damage and con-
trol costs. CITRUS RUST MITE (Phyllocoptruta oleivora) was of general
occurrence in 2 southern counties, being widespread and more numerous than in 5
past years in San Diego County where it did over $200,000 in damage.
CALIFORNIA RED SCALE (Aonidiella aurantii) was a serious economic factor in
citrus in southern counties. Infestations in Los Angeles County were heavier
than in 1956, but control was good in most areas. BLACK SCALE (Saissetia oleae)
was general, ranging light to heavy with marked increases noted in San Diego
County. OLIVE SCALE (Parlatoria oleae) caused over $200,000 damage to citrus
in San Diego County and was locally prevalent on peaches and apricots in Los
Angeles County. General and above normal heavy populations of CITRUS MEALYBUG
(Pseudococcus citri) developed in a few coastal San Diego County groves and was
general in Los Angeles County with occasional spot damage. CITRUS THRIPS
(Scirtothrips citri) was prevalent in 5 southern counties with damage to new
growth more evident in San Diego County than usual, with no commercial loss.
There was moderate damage to some Los Angeles County lemon orchards where an
increased total acreage was treated. Black citrus aphid, spirea aphid, green
peach aphid and melon aphid were heavier on citrus in Los Angeles County

necessitating treatment of some 850 acres. GREEN PEACH APHID (Myzus persicae) and POTATO APHID (Macrosiphum solanifolii) were abundant on orange trees in San Diego County in March-April but damage was light.

Truck Crop Insects: CUTWORMS AND ARMYWORMS damaged truck and garden crops in north central areas and were reported on truck crops from most southern areas. BLACK CUTWORM (Agrotis ypsilon) was generally distributed over Yolo County developing medium populations on tomatoes. In Yolo County BEET ARMYWORM (Laphygma frugiperda) was of limited significance on beets. Infestations built up to medium on garbanzo beans in Los Angeles County and heavy populations occurred generally on Imperial County sugar beets. SALT-MARSH CATERPILLAR (Estigmene acrea) damage was generally localized in 5 central coastal counties, ranging from light to severe. Populations were general in 3 southern counties with light to heavy damage on cauliflower, beans, celery, beets and miscellaneous crops with nearly $1,000,000 damage in the Imperial Valley. CORN EARWORM (Heliothis zea) damaged tomatoes, corn, lettuce and bell peppers in 7 central coastal counties. In the Sacramento Valley, distribution was general with light to locally heavy infestations on tomatoes and corn. General light to medium infestations were damaging in 6 counties of the San Joaquin Valley. In southern counties this insect infested tomatoes, corn, beans and lettuce; populations varying to heavy. State-wide costs amounted to $15,831,975 in 1957.

POTATO TUBERWORM (Gnorimoschema operculella) infestations were generally slight to moderate in Monterey County. In the adjoining counties of San Benito and San Luis Obispo infestations were localized but severe, with control and damage totaling $91,440. Damage by ARTICHOKE PLUME MOTH (Platyptilia carduidactyla) to artichoke in Santa Cruz, Monterey and San Luis Obispo Counties was generally localized, with the last 2 counties estimating loss and control costs at $550,750. Although of limited distribution in Santa Barbara County, this insect caused an estimated $44,000 loss to artichoke growers. ALFALFA LOOPER (Autographa californica) and CABBAGE LOOPER (Trichoplusia ni) were among the more important insect pests in the State during 1957. Infestations were light to moderate in central coastal counties. Medium damage occurred to lettuce crops in western Stanislaus County in September and cabbage and celery were damaged in the Manteca area of San Joaquin County. These 2 loopers were prevalent throughout southern counties on truck crops. Cabbage looper has become the most injurious pest of vegetable crops in Los Angeles County, with $80,000 spent for control during 1957. Combined, these 2 species caused estimated losses of $3,900,000 in these areas.

LESSER CORNSTALK BORER (Elasmopalpus lignosellus) was of some concern on sorghums, corn and beans in Riverside and Imperial Counties. TOMATO PINWORM (Keiferia lycopersicella) was generally light with heavy damage in some fall tomato plantings in the Chula Vista area of San Diego County. Losses were estimated at $571,900.

TWO-SPOTTED SPIDER MITE (Tetrancyhus telarius) populations in the San Joaquin Valley were light to heavy with considerable damage to San Joaquin County crops. TOMATO RUSSET MITE (Vasates lycopersici) was general on tomato plantings in Sacramento and Yolo Counties. Occurrence was general over Los Angeles and local in Riverside Counties, neither reporting much damage. Summer migrations of CLOVER MITE (Bryobia praetiosa) to pole beans in San Diego County necessitated some control. SPIDER MITES damaged beans in Fresno County, and Kings and Stanislaus Counties experienced damage from general, light to moderate infestations. Locally medium to heavy populations of mites developed on field corn and beans in Tehama County.

GREEN PEACH APHID (Myzus persicae) damaged peppers in Merced County and heavy populations occurred in the Linden area of San Joaquin County. Potatoes were damaged in Kern County. This aphid, along with pea aphid, caused enough

injury to vegetables to be classed as one of the more important insects in Santa
Barbara County. Estimated damage and control costs were $300,000. CABBAGE
APHID (Brevicoryne brassicae) was reported from 4 central coastal counties
where damage was assessed at $288,700. The aphid required controls in
Sacramento County,infested crucifers generally in several southern counties
with light to heavy damage. MELON APHID (Aphis gossypii) caused extensive
damage to watermelons in areas of Stanislaus and San Joaquin Counties and was
among the more important insect pests in 2 southern counties, damaging miscellaneous vegetables and orange trees. APHID populations were light to medium in
Tulare County and damaging in Stanislaus and Fresno Counties. Anuraphis
apiifoliae developed to a problem on celery in January and February in coastal
San Diego County, and Sappaphis foeniculus caused heavy damage to carrots in the
Tracy area of San Joaquin County.

In the San Joaquin Valley GRASSHOPPERS caused some light to medium damage to
truck crops. FIELD CRICKET (Acheta assimilis) damaged new transplants of tomatoes and eggplants in Merced County. BEET LEAFHOPPER (Circulifer tenellus) was
generally light over Tulare County. LYGUS BUGS (Lygus spp.) caused an estimated
damage of $125,000 on beans in Monterey County. Populations were locally impor-
tant on various crops in the Sacramento Valley. Infestations were mostly
general in some southern counties with considerable damage in untreated bean
fields in Los Angeles County. LEAF MINERS (Liriomyza spp. and Agromyza spp.)
damaged peas, lettuce, celery, spinach and crucifers in 5 central coastal
counties, with Monterey County suffering an estimated $11,630,000 damage to
these crops. Populations developed in a wide variety of crops in 4 southern
counties. Fairly heavy populations developed on Imperial County tomatoes.
Beans in the Palo Verde Valley of Riverside County were severely attacked. PEA
LEAF MINER (L. langei) heavily mined truck crops in Monterey County during the
population peak in late June and July. SEED-CORN MAGGOT (Hylemya cilicrura)
caused light to medium damage in Riverside, Santa Barbara and Los Angeles
Counties. WESTERN SPOTTED CUCUMBER BEETLE (Diabrotica undecimpunctata) was
light to severe in Tulare County requiring control measures. Diabrotica spp.
were general in 2 southern counties. VEGETABLE WEEVIL (Listroderes
costirostris obliquus) was light in Santa Barbara, Riverside and Los Angeles
Counties. PEPPER WEEVIL (Anthonomus eugenii) caused damage to pepper plantings
in San Diego County in the amount of $110,690. WIREWORMS moderately damaged the
potato crop in areas of San Joaquin County and caused some damage to crops in
Santa Barbara, Riverside and Los Angeles Counties. EUROPEAN EARWIG (Forficula
auricularia) damaged field and garden plants in the Stockton area of San
Joaquin County and heavy populations of PAVEMENT ANT (Tetramorium caespitum)
were very damaging to tomatoes in the Tracy area of the same county. WHITE-
FLIES required treatment in Fresno County, with no extent of damage reported.

Cotton Insects: LYGUS BUGS (Lygus spp.) were general in Tulare County ranging
from light to severe. Madera County reported a general light infestation.
There was considerable damage in Kings County. These insects were general in
the Imperial Valley with heavy populations developing and causing considerable
damage, amounting to approximately $1,500,000. Medium populations developed
in the Palo Verde Valley of Riverside County. Damage to cotton in Imperial
County was estimated at $917,000 from lygus as well as from STINK BUGS. Heavy
damage occurred in all areas of the San Joaquin Valley from infestation by
BOLLWORM (Heliothis zea) and populations were general. Damage to cotton in
Riverside, Los Angeles and Imperial Counties was light to heavy. Damage by
SPIDER MITES was moderate in Madera County. Infestations were light to severe
in Tulare County and required controls in Fresno County. Extensive control was
necessary in Kings County. In the southern counties damage occurred locally,
with heavy populations developing in Imperial County. TWO-SPOTTED SPIDER MITE
(Tetranychus telarius) built up to a medium infestation in the Coachella Valley
of Riverside County. APHIDS and GRASSHOPPERS required control in Fresno County.
Light grasshopper damage occurred in Kern County and Madera County reported

moderate populations attacking all crops generally. COTTON LEAF PERFORATOR
(Bucculatrix thurberiella) caused considerable damage to cotton in Imperial
County and was medium to heavy in Riverside County.

Forest, Ornamental and Shade Tree Insects: Severe damage was caused to home
plantings of spruce by SPRUCE NEEDLE MINER (Taniva albolineana) in the Alturas
area of Modoc County. .A PLANT BUG (Neoborus illitus) caused severe defoliation
of ash trees in 3 central coastal counties, being recorded for the first time
in San Luis Obispo County. Infestations of ELM LEAF BEETLE (Galerucella
xanthomelaena) were moderate to severe on ornamental elms in central coastal
counties, with general defoliations to unsprayed trees. In the Sacramento
Valley considerable defoliation occurred on untreated trees. Damage was severe
to elms generally in Tulare County. Severe destruction was curbed by sprays in
Tuolumne and Calaveras Counties and infestations in Los Angeles County were
locally heavy on elms. A CARNATION BUD MITE (Aceria paradianthi) was reported
for the first time from San Mateo and Alameda Counties on carnations. Survey
uncovered infestations in 13 glasshouse plantings in Alameda, San Mateo and
Santa Clara Counties.

BROWN-HEADED ASH SAWFLY (Tomostethus multicinctus) was locally heavy on ash in
Tehama County and an ASH TINGID (Leptoypha minor) occurred generally over Yolo
County and was a problem in the Escalon area of San Joaquin County. SMALLER
EUROPEAN ELM BARK BEETLE (Scolytus multistriatus) was taken for first time in
Sacramento County in elm logs of unknown origin and later determined to be
killing elms in certain sections of the city of Sacramento. A SPRUCE APHID
(Cinara piceicola) was taken for a first State record on Norway spruce in San
Bernardino County and was also found in El Dorado County. In Tulare County
COTTONY-CUSHION SCALE (Icerya purchasi) was light to medium on ornamentals
and OLIVE SCALE (Parlatoria oleae) damaged ornamentals. Locally heavy populations of TWO-SPOTTED SPIDER MITE (Tetranychus telarius) built up on San
Bernardino County shade trees. LESSER CORNSTALK BORER (Elasmopalpus
lignosellus) heavily attacked flowering tops of papyrus in San Diego County,
which is an unusual host for this pest. RHODES-GRASS SCALE (Antonina
graminis) was taken in Imperial County heavily infesting St. Augustine grass
and a SCALE (Aspidiotus candidula) was taken on mesquite and mistletoe in
Imperial County, both constituting first State records. MOURNING-CLOAK
BUTTERFLY (Nymphalis antiopa) was generally troublesome on poplars and elms,
among other trees, in San Diego County in the spring. A PSYLLID (Euphyllura
arbuti) built up heavy populations on native madrone in the Ukiah-Talmage area
of Mendocino County and infestations of an OAK TREEHOPPER (Platycotis vittata)
were medium generally throughout the same area.

Insects Affecting Man and Animals: CAT and DOG FLEAS were a nuisance in some
areas of the Sacramento Valley. BLACK WIDOW SPIDER (Latrodectus mactans) was
of concern to householders and a buildup of HOUSE FLY (Musca domestica) and a
VINEGAR FLY (Drosophila melanogaster) occurred in Sacramento in the fall.

Stored-Product Insects: Specimens of a DERMESTID (Thylodrias contractus)
collected in a San Diego warehouse are a first State record, with a second
record from Imperial County. Another DERMESTID (Perimegatoma vespulae) was
collected for the second time in the State in Ventura County. A GRAIN MOTH
(Endrosis lacteella) was taken in stored grain in Los Angeles County.

Beneficial Insects: Insects that aid in the suppression of agricultural crop pests were in evidence in many parts of the State. Praon palitans, Trioxys utilis and Aphelinus semiflavus were liberated for spotted alfalfa aphid control in many areas of the State. P. palitans is the most widespread species having been established well up to the northern end of the Sacramento Valley and generally over the southern part of the State. COCCINELLIDS and GREEN LACEWINGS did an excellent job in many areas. PARASITES and PREDATORS reduced treatment costs in several counties. Parasites of red scale were noted doing an excellent job in San Diego County. Four species were involved, Aphytis chrysomphali, A. lingnanensis, Comperiella bifasciata, and Prospaltella perniciosi, the last-named species was also found in Orange County outnumbering A. chrysomphali in a number of groves. Various black scale parasites showed a marked increase over the past 2 years in San Diego County although in Orange County they were less effective than in former seasons. The PURPLE SCALE PARASITE (Aphytis lepidosaphes) continues to be effective in Orange County. Cryptolaemus montrouzieri predatory on citrus mealybug, is reared and released by several counties in Southern California. Over 48,000,000 individuals were handled in this manner in the last year. KLAMATHWEED BEETLES (Chrysolina hyperici and C. gemellata) were active throughout their range on Klamathweed or St. Johns wort and are continuing to hold down spread of this noxious weed.

Insect Loss Estimates for California - 1957

Reported by R. M. Hawthorne

Insects	Estimated Damage & Loss	Insects	Estimated Damage & Loss
Aphids-General	$ 9,191,770	Cabbage and alfalfa	$ 4,014,108
Apple aphid	100,000	loopers	
Cabbage aphid	523,700		
Green peach aphid		Lygus bugs	3,083,764
and pea aphid	393,744		
Hop aphid	34,000	Cotton leaf	
Rosy apple aphid	150,000	perforator	1,834,887
Sugar-beet root aphid	120,000		
Spotted alfalfa aphid	9,704,627	Leafhoppers-general and	
Woolly apple aphid	50,200	grape leafhopper	
Walnut aphid	162,000	(Erythroneura sp.)	884,101
Cotton aphid	460,000		
Aphids - Total	20,890,041	Leaf miners:	
		Liriomyza sp.	25,000
Alfalfa caterpillar	781,635	Liriomyza langei	12,377,500
		Hydrellia griseola	15,000
Artichoke plume moth	594,750	Leaf miners - Total	12,417,500
Armyworms:		Navel orangeworm	230,960
Beet armyworm	15,821,175		
Western yellow-		Potato tuberworm	1,586,440
striped armyworm	10,800		
Armyworms-Total	15,831,975	Peach twig borer	2,979,176
Borers:		Pear psylla	12,000
Pacific flatheaded			
borer, flatheaded		Spider mites-General	3,258,525
apple tree borer,		Brown wheat mite	10,000
Western peach tree		Citrus red mite	2,813,920
borer	56,200	Clover mite	392,300
		European red mite	107,500
Corn earworm	15,047,188	Two-spotted spider mite	997,425
		Spider mites - Total	7,579,670
Codling moth	828,530		

Imported cabbageworm	15,000
Pear-slug	90
Cutworms-General	833,225
Dark-sided cutworm	1,000
Cutworms - Total	834,225
European earwig	1,665
Cattle grubs	4,000
Western spotted cucumber beetle	521,531
Snowy tree cricket	40
Grasshoppers	1,704,977
Field crickets and grasshoppers	4,021,020
(Estimate Imperial County 1957)	
Grape leaf folder	209,510
Thrips-General	155,448
Onion thrips	45,000
Pear thrips	20,000
Thrips - Total	220,448
Alfalfa weevil	121,800
Pepper weevil	110,690
Lesser clover leaf weevil	1,000
Granary weevil	10,000

Cyclamen mite	1,940,555
Citrus rust mite	218,920
Grape erineum mite	135,000
Eriophyid mites - Total	2,294,475
Sheep ked	1,500
Black scale	100,000
European fruit lecanium	125,000
A frosted scale (Lecanium pruinosum)	90,000
Olive scale	55,465
Purple scale	780,000
California red scale	3,200,000
San Jose scale	645,264
Scales - Total	4,995,729
Stink Bugs - General and Consperse stink bug	1,115,101
Salt-marsh caterpillar	866,725
Tomato pinworm	406,600
Tent caterpillar (Malacosoma sp.)	14,000
Whiteflies	18,040
Darkling ground beetles	52,500
Weevils (Brachyrhinus sp.)	1,803,000
Wireworms	401,125
GRAND TOTAL	$108,397,716

A MITE NOT KNOWN TO OCCUR IN THE UNITED STATES

RED-LEGGED EARTH MITE (Halotydeus destructor Tucker)

Economic Importance: This mite is a serious pest of vegetables and other crops, especially seedlings, in South Africa, Australia and parts of New Zealand. It is one of the chief pests of clover pastures in areas of Australia. Enormous numbers are often found on subterranean clover (Trifolium subterraneum) in that country. The mites hatch at same time as clover seeds germinate and feed heavily on the seedlings. Young clover, potatoes, tomatoes, lettuce and peas are often stunted or killed. The pest also invades greenhouses and total destruction of tomato seedlings in such locations has been recorded in the Adelaide area. Foliage of heavily attacked older plants rapidly wilts and shrivels, finally appearing scorched

Damage to Clover

Distribution: Australia, New Zealand, South Africa.

Hosts: Attacks many plants, broad-leaved preferred. Among the more important hosts are clovers, potato, tomato, tobacco, peas, beans, lettuce, and beets.

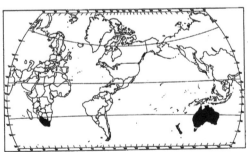

General Distribution of Red-Legged Earth Mite

Eupodidae, Acarina

314

Life History and Habits: In Australia the mite is active in autumn, winter and spring and passes the summer in egg stage, when other stages succumb to higher temperature and dessication. Eggs hatch in late April and May and a large population develops which frequently causes severe damage to seedlings. Infestations dwindle by early June but become high again in July and remain so to the middle of October. Oviposition occurs mostly on undersides of hosts, in damp situations where plants are near or in contact with soil. Eggs are deposited in a single layer and no webbing is present. The mites are gregarious feeders on all parts of low-growing plants. Light, sandy soils and cool, rainy weather favor development of infestations.

Description: Adult has velvety black body and red legs. Integument has very fine striae. Double row of feathered setae on dorsal surface near the mid-line. Plumose setae also on legs and ventral surface. First pair of legs longest, second shortest. Legs terminate in paired claws and median pulvilli. Two ocelli on antero-lateral margins of body. Anus terminal, genital aperture is ventral. Genital aperture large, flanked by two suckers and numerous setae. Mouthparts subterminal, palps five-jointed, chelicerae short and powerful, hypostome strongly muscular, bifurcate, terminating in chitinous papillae. Body length about 1 mm. Egg oval, less than 0.2 mm. long, bright yellow or orange. Smooth and shining when moist but whitish when dry. Young larva more elongated than adult, segmentation distinct. Nymphs assume black coloring of adults few days after hatching. (Prepared in Plant Pest Survey Section in cooperation with other ARS agencies.) CEIR 8(16) 4-18-58

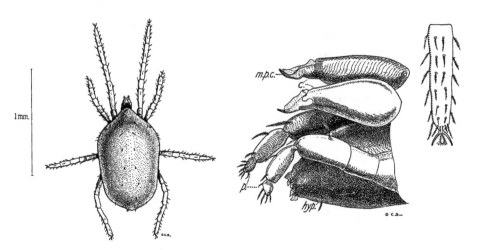

Halotydeus destructor Adult   Mouth Parts and Fore-tarsus

Figures (except map) from Swan, D. C. 1934. Jour. Dept. Agr. (South Australia) 38(3):353-367.

Lightning Source UK Ltd.
Milton Keynes UK
UKHW020913220119
335965UK00013B/1882/P